AF610641

This is a letter in the form of a book

Keeping The Best For Last

Published by Sami Desormeaux
https://www.theofficialsami.com

Edited by Sami Desormeaux
Cover by Sami Desormeaux
Islamic leaf design by Sami Desormeaux

With thanks to Akel Kahera and Azizah Kahera for the Family images

Copyright Registration Number:
1189149
Canadian ISBN:
978-1-7770420-4-2

Canadian Intellectual Property Office:
Place du Portage I
50 Victoria Street
Gatineau, QC, Canada
K1A 0C9

First Canadian Edition: January 2022
Digitally uploaded in Canada

Grand-maman, in honour of your passing thirteen years ago, may you be proud of your grand-children. Je t'aime!

Keeping The Best For Last

Sami

Dedicated to my wife

Wedding Vows

May you be at peace with the words below, being my wedding vows to you

My sweetest love,

as I gaze into the infinite skies, I see a world beyond any imagining or reckoning. Such a timeless thought appears to so quickly pass by. It is only by looking through this immense darkness that I see the gracious brilliance of the stars. This light is precious, as every second passes through the night, the darkness grows until it knows no bounds.

This same beauty from the skies, I witness it as I glance over towards you and look into your eyes. Beholding it, there is a poignant melody dancing in the starry moonlight, within the white of your eyes. And like an awe-inspiring supernova embracing the night, so too my own eyes shower you with emboldened affection.

So, it is within the romantic storms that engulf our hearts, that I promise you that I will be as honest as I can be. For every word spoken to you, a single heartbeat will follow continuously even though I may not be the greatest man. Yet, I know that I am the perfect person which your heart desires. As I search for the key to your heart, I will stand by its awe-inspiring gate awaiting that your emotions flood your crimson soul, so that the gates to it will open.

Before the tide is overwhelmed by love, I will stand by your side ever so valiantly. Should I ever lose heart or courage, I will utter every word that is imprinted within my spirit, so that your calm voice may appease me with serenity. I will cherish your words, as you soothe my every thought and my every concern.

The ghost of your soul haunts my dreams and my mind, in a peaceful way. As you clutch my mind and even my body, I feel the soothing embrace of your own soul as it melds with mine as one.

From the time we met, we were so far from one another. Yet, even as you are now in my embrace, I still feel deep sorrow within my heart. I miss you beyond belief, especially when you are with me. I wish I could tell you how much I desire you to a greater extent, as I gaze into your soulful eyes.

As I think of you, all I want is to be in your grasp. I love you no matter what. There will never come a time where I will love you "even if", because there will only be times when I love you "no matter what". I have waited so long to be with you, and longed for you. I have spent nearly thirty years searching endless nights, while dreaming about the day I would find you.

In the end, as in the beginning, it was distance which brought us closer. To shorten that gap, I had to open my heart like never before; more than ever with somebody else.

Ultimately, as the storm rages within the shy prowess of your sweet laughter, I become emboldened to know that I can find solace within you, in the lands of "Zeinabia". To lose myself forevermore, as I drown in the peaceful embrace that is you.

We may have disagreements with each other, but I'll be the one capable of supporting you the way you need to be supported personally and in your faith. I will be the fiery guardian of your tears, as well as the perfect flaw within your dreamy eyes. Inside the inner workings of those milky white eyes, you shall dream a dream. As a finger touching water, I shall be the reflection upon the surface of your eyes.

Whenever you gaze at yourself in the mirror, you shall see me in a dreamlike manner. I will be the rock upon water, creating a reflection that is surreal. It is when you shall fail that I will lend you my strength, so that you may preserve the stillness of your thoughts.

Remember that whenever my heart melts for you, it is because I recall the reason I love you. Your uniquely sumptuous smile recites a thousand and one love stories, as you utter honeyed words. It is like the embrace of your arms and the clasp of your hands upon my face, where your voice claims the beauty of the paired gems that reflects the light off of your own.

The shadow of your milky eyes gaze into mine, forevermore trapped within a flawed perfection. It is this unbeholden look that is woven within me, binding the shadow of your eyes to me, for I hold the darkness and the lightness of your heart. Be they awe-inspiring beauties or dreadful moments that cling unto your spirit. Whether into light or darkness, you are my world.

You are more than that, you are the secret Sixth Pillar of Islam – one of the most important gems of this world has your name. To remind myself of all I hold dear, I look back at the cufflinks I bought for our wedding. As I see the initials of your name upon my sleeve, it reminds me that I always keep the best for last, Z as in Zeinab.

On the previous page were the wedding vows I had written for you. I have often wondered how I could make them better, as they were never enough. Not for me, despite the tears or the smiles they brought on others. How do you create a masterpiece when the person it's written for deserves more than that? I wish I had an answer for that, as I have continuously worked on those vows to make them better.

Years later, I still wish I had the ability to create a tapestry of words for you. The hardest thing is knowing I have the capacity, without understanding how to improve what seems like a life's work, despite the shortness of it.

Strangely enough, one of the reasons I've never creatively written in French was because I never saw the point of writing in a language where its beauty existed already. Whereas the English language is rougher around the edges and more to the point.

Enriching such a dialect within an intense sea of languages is much more complex. To soar above such an intricate one is a miracle in and of itself. To weave words together when there is nothing more complicated, is to be an artist that possesses raw talent.

Perhaps this is the reason that I time and again fail to lay ink on paper. How can I tell you how much I appreciate you when words could never suffice? They can be powerful, as well as devastating. They can be anything you wish for them to be. Most importantly, they can also be insufficient and weak.

Where can I start? Where does this odyssey even begin? I never imagined myself getting married, and even less for as long as we have been married thus far. What I do know is that we have, in such a short time span, experienced a lifetime's worth of pain. We have lost so much, and we had to watch each other tremendously suffer. Yet, for all of our negative experiences in this life, the only way for us is up.

To imagine worse things that could occur, we are strong enough to soar to better heights. At least, I hope so, with all that we've experienced in a small amount of time. Still, for all of our dreams, aspirations and desires, we have yet to defeat our greatest fears. Whatever they may be, we have each other. While I may be the wings that carry you while you need me, I know you are the same.

Those terrible fears are almost like dreaded apparitions that no one else sees, except you. The weakness within is a manifestation of that, and conquering the darkness is not an easy thing to do. They make us afraid, or make us do or say things out of fright. We both know what that means, yet at times, it's easier to give in to that fright, than to stand tall and see through the darkness.

The moment we use the tools that Allah has given us to rise above a mediocre self, is the instant we stop listening to the Shaytan (Satan). It will always be easier to be frightened, or simply do and say things we don't mean. The truth is that we all make decisions every day, and I know that I have become a better person because of you. It may not always seem that way, but I can't imagine anyone else being the reflection in the mirror of my soul.

It may be true that only we can believe in ourselves, and that no one else can in our stead. Yet, it always helps having the greatest person be there for you. I know that for a fact, as I got married to her (you). If truth be told, there are times where I wish I could believe in myself the same way you do with me, and I know for a fact you wish the same at times.

There is never a moment where we fully believe in ourselves. There will always be doubt, because as my favourite saying goes: To err is human. In and of itself, this is the reason we have each other - when one of us falters, the other is there to help out. Every single moment we've refused the other's help, or that we've known better than the other, were all instants of forgetting to believe in ourselves and each other.

The torments within and without are what drives us to shudder in the corner. Regardless, you, like me, have the potential to be the same person that you coach others to be. No matter where you are in life, I will be there to catch you should you fall. After all, to be divinely inspired once is to be so for as long as possible. I will always remind you of your potential and greatness.

Perhaps the days we have spent becoming who we are was to allow us to thereafter ponder for decades, not who we could become, but rather who we failed to be. There is no escape from the past or the future. We are the creation of our parents' fears, hopes and influence.

A Reflection Of Our Parents

Our parents are but a mirror of our soul, to let us know what lies beyond our selves

As you know, I was once speaking to my father via my webcam, and I began hysterically laughing... well ok, not hysterically, but quite a bit. He then asked what was so funny, to which I answered, as I pointed at him, “that’s me in thirty years”.

As if that wasn’t enough, when I was around eighteen, I was in the elevator with my father. The janitor greeted my dad while looking at me, doing so using my father’s name. My father then leaned forward, looked to his left and greeted him back, confusing him for a brief moment. If that isn’t someone confusing you for your parent... I don’t know what is.

All of this to say that we are a product of who our parents either wanted us to be, or who they are hoping we will be. But most importantly, we are the product of generations of people that we look like.

They are the first people we look up to or emulate, simply because they are the ones who look out for us. We often end up behaving in a similar manner, while hoping to become a better version not of ourselves, but of them. Allah aside in terms of ultimate creation power, we are literally a creation of our parents on a molecular level. We therefore become a version of them, one that we hope soars higher than they have.

All that said, when do we stop being our parents and be ourselves instead? All the times I have called you by your mother’s name because you acted the same way your mother did, that is not a coincidence. I know it sounds funny at times in those situations, but at the same time you have to realize that you have to be yourself.

Do not be a watered down version that's not you, not to say that your mother was a watered down version of herself. She was a full version of herself, or at least I hope so. I would love to see the closest version of who Zeinab is. All of this to say that love isn't about the written romance or fantasies. It's about growing older, together.

That moment of clarity when you realize you're not an adult is when you see children playing sports, and they have more sportsmanship than professional players as that don't purposely dive or take an "easy" fall, unlike the so called pros (or con artists if you prefer). Then it dawns on us that we are not adults when we can't even act that way. And so, as we figure that out and start growing up, there is nothing more terrifying than thinking that we are legally adults.

That day when we say, "oh my God... Can you believe we are adults?" is the same day we understand that we are royally screwed. Why? Because we have never prepared for that day. Perhaps this is why we have each other, so we can grow. Our experiences, as well as how and when they occurred, are never going to be the same. Still, having each other is the best thing that can happen, since that is how we grow up, by growing old together. On top of that, we can look out for each other and always be an unwavering flag, steadfast for the other.

I realize that you have had more time than me to grow by yourself, as you've always been much more independent than I have. Within the confines of this life, you may always be a step ahead of me. I understand it's not going to always be easy for you, and that you wish for me to be more. I've already grown a lot because of you, not despite of you.

I've often wondered who I was, and where I was heading in life. If not for you, I may never have seen the reality of who I am. You've done more for me than my parents combined, not because of their lack of love or devotion, but because you helped me to understand better who I was. I certainly owe you a lot, though I don't know how or if I could ever repay that debt. If anything, I've only started my life in my late thirties.

I can only hope to give you as much as you have given me thus far. Perhaps one day I will be fortunate enough to make you see the greatness in yourself. Which, in your case, is already past your potential. You do things I could only dream of having the courage to do. You have no idea how blessed you are to have such a fuller range of independence and belief in yourself.

Whatever you do in this life, just know that I truly am proud of you. I do mean it when I say that. I see the talents I have, at least the ones I am aware of. As for you, I wish I had yours sometimes. Not out of jealousy, but rather out of a sense of desire to be a better self. I may not agree with the term "a better version of yourself", as there is only one unique version. But, I do see the value of becoming better, both for you and myself.

Obviously, we will disappoint each other more often at times. If anything, it's due to the fact that we care enough about what the other person thinks more than anyone else. I get that, and I feel disappointed when I let you down. I would like to do better, despite knowing I can't always be at my greatest all the time. But you know what? We can always become better, and older in the process. I'm not sure how I feel about the latter though.

On top of this, I would like for you to see both of us as good as we can be. It may take a while, as the road is always treacherous when we insist on driving on it. Nonetheless, there is always gold at the end of the rainbow. If that last part was true, we'd be rich. Well... At least we can have rich hearts. That was corny, though knowing you, I'm sure it's something you appreciated.

Your outlook on life is certainly different than mine, yet I can't imagine sharing my life with anyone else despite our differences. A part of me wish I could have the same understanding in life that you have, although I also can't imagine not being who I am. The subtle nature of our souls is ever so delicate. Mine is an everlasting abundance of youth, where I see the world through soulful eyes. Yet, I see the world for what it is, instead of what I'd want it to be as a younger person.

Whenever I think about what I see in this world, I am always so bitterly reminded of a bygone era that I loved so much. The music, the computers and their archaic operating systems, as well as the amazing stories told through the lens of eighties and nineties movies. It's not even nostalgia, but a way of life. At times, I wish I could escape all that and see the world for what it shows me as it peers inside me.

I may not always understand or comprehend why you see things the way you see them, as I am baffled at times. Regardless, I couldn't imagine loving you less because of who I fail to be as I try to walk into a modern world. Perhaps I am trying to be someone that so desperately seeks to see the future in a post-modern way, where the past and future is one. This may not make sense to you, but it does to me.

The sacrifices we have made thus far are based on trying to accept the other's flaws and way of thinking as much as possible. That doesn't have to mean that we would have to be so different as to be indifferent about each other. If anything, I wish to learn to obtain your strengths, and you mine.

It's true that there are moments where I don't always know how to be the great person you see me at times. I'm still learning so much, as the world around me has always been so different compared to me. One day, I hope to be the person I'd like for you to look at. I only want to be better, since there is no reason to settle for a lesser self.

What I do know is that we are all looking for something in this life. The question is always: What are we looking for? I'm looking for a semblance of normality within Sami's World, where I'm still able to become someone greater than how I currently see myself as. Hopefully I will be able to find myself, so that you don't have to. I try to be the best that I can be, even when it's not obvious to anyone else.

I'll often struggle to do so many things because I have Asperger's, but I still want to see a flawless reflection of myself in your eyes. There is nothing more important than to become as amazing as I'd like to be. After all, time on Earth is so limited, that we don't even realize this or fathom how short of a time we have. Before you know it, we grow taller and move on with our lives away from our families.

There lies life itself, in the depth of a grain of sand within the universe. Where we falter, fall, rise and seek out a world for ourselves from this tiny rock. It may not be easy to walk this earth without a greater purpose or a deen (path in life), but there comes a moment where our limited time here asks us to look at this planet and the people around it. Finding that one person within eight billion others is truly a feat in and of itself.

To assume we are good enough or more so than the other when it comes to being with them would be arrogant. It is in our transition from a very young adult life into a "middle ground", right before midlife, that we realize how lost we are. We end up growing up a second time, despite our age. We've had to endure countless waves of hardships, for better or worse. Whatever happens, just know that I love you.

The wondrous galaxy that is contained within life couldn't be complete without you in it for better or worse, even when the universe itself is limitless. The sky is the limit, or rather those infinite grains of "sand" are. Being able to imagine and ponder upon the marvels of this world, can only be done through the eyes of our inner child.

As we reconcile the fact that we are more than a single person, we realize that we are an adult with an inner child inside us. However long it takes, I'll be waiting for that inner child in you to pop out, as I'd like to show you the wonders of the world... Be it the past, the future, the stars, or anything in between. And then, maybe you can get the inner adult in me, or just the adult that is me to grow even more.

Inspirational Pillar

To move and be moved,
To be and to become,
To be strength itself
Is to become immovable

We both know that I've always marvelled at the universe, as well as what I see as an inevitable future. I may not know everything in this world nor how to do everything, yet I know that everything is possible. Where there is a will, there is always a way. After all, our own social history has proved changes in science, fashion, technology, food and so much more exist. As the saying goes, "necessity is the mother of invention". Or perhaps, a gaze at the stars was what it took for humankind to desire more in this life.

All of that to say how much we have to live or cry for. It's not always going to be easy, despite the tools we have. Just know that we don't live life for others, but we can only grow because of others, and our desire to want more. When we get upset or become either happy or sad, it's a manifestation of our emotions. Those, believe it or not, are merely our inner child feeling frustration at and in that situation.

I know for a fact that we both get on each other's nerves at times, but we look at creating beautiful things for the other as well. Whether it's a night out, or just a simple conversation, it's always something to look forward to.

At the end of the day despite anything and everything, you are my inspiration, my muse and the Sixth Pillar of Islam. A gift from Allah which has helped me on my deen to become a better person all around, while helping me discover more of who I am. To have such a gift from Allah is truly a blessing. I may not always see it, but I know that it's the simple truth. Because of you, I am a husband, a father and I hope a better individual because of it all.

Weathering the storm that is life, you are truly a pillar in every possible sense, making all of this simpler. It's never been clear to navigate this world, yet you've made it easier for me to have a better life. I know I've taught you a lot of things in life as well, but none that compares to all the positive things I've had in mine because of you. Even when the world stops for you, I realize that you forget yourself within that storm. In those moments, I remind you who you are.

I remind you that you are not your mother, but your own person. Someone that has accomplished so much in life, and made sure others could become better. Not for others, but simply for themselves, as only they can become subsequently better for themselves and others afterwards. You are that triumph within a world void of goodness, as you always want to see the positive in every situation.

On this earth, people will only remember what you brought them, not the failures that haunts you on a daily basis. We both may look at the negative more often than we should, and that is what brings us down more often than not. Inside this torment, there is always a way out, so we should strive to reach for a better world. I know it won't always be easy, but we have to see the beauties within us. Those are the things which enables us to reach for the stars, instead of aiming for something lesser than that.

I see you as a pillar of inspiration, as do so many people. Every time you bring yourself down equates to you denying the praises from those who believe in you. Most importantly, it denies Allah's own praise for you through those same people, as He's the only one who truly knows who you are.

On top of that, as Maya Angelou said, "[i]f I am not good to myself, how can I expect anyone else to be good to me?" Remember to love and respect yourself as much as others do. It's not easy, I know. Doubt is our greatest nemesis, not fear. The seeds of doubt can instill that fear that we so dread both feeling and, ironically, fearing.

Due to your efforts, dedication, and raw talent, you have brought the best out of people. Regardless of whether people agree with you or not, things you accomplish are not meant to deter or discourage others. The belief in ourselves is the hardest to believe in, despite those outside clamoring about our own disbeliefs.

If truth be told, you know how to inspire others in a manner that places the rest of us to shame. That's not a bad thing of course, as it shows us how we should strive to emulate you. There are many days where I wish I could be the same as you in so many ways.

When my grandmother was alive, she was the pillar of the household. There was something about her quiet and kind-hearted personality that people loved. You may not be like her in terms of who she was, as you are certainly more boisterous than she ever was. Yet, you demonstrate the same pillar-like mentality. Something most people could never possess, but not for lack of trying. Like my grandmother, you are an outlier in that regard, since being this way is a real gift.

I realize it won't always be easy for you to be that, as being the pillar of a family is never a given status but a mere fact of life. Just like my grandmother who had our grandfather, rest assured that I will always be there for you. Sure, I will probably stumble and falter... Ok, probably a lot, but that's why we have each other.

In the end, a literal pillar is meant to both support and be supported by what is underneath it. I hope we will be able and capable of being there for each other. After all, when I see some of the people we know, they too have been through hell and back. Yet, they have always been there for each other. The sense of community found around the family pillar is immense, and a power to be reckoned with.

Knowing you, you'll most likely deny being the person I know you are. To which I would reply, "you can't take a compliment now, can you?". Although, that sounds more like something you would say to me. If anything, believe me when I say that no one compares to the person you are. I did get married to you, after all.

Whenever you have a doubt about anything and especially about yourself, just remember that there isn't anyone like you. Considering there are eight billion people on earth, that says a lot as no fingerprint is the same. You are unique, as much as I am. Yet, I know the person you are has to be the best person for me. Of which I hope I am for you as well.

You inspire me to try harder, or simply try. It's never easy or pleasant, but when I AM able to look back at what I accomplish, I am thankful to you. I understand the process to get there is often frustrating and so damn annoying. Yet, once I'm there at the top of the hill, I realize I've accomplished something much greater than what I set myself out to do. I couldn't do it without you, not because I'm incapable of it, but rather it makes it easier having someone believing in you when no one really ever voiced those words of encouragement.

Even since I had voiced goals I had in mind, I've always wanted to accomplish those. Having a second person not only reinforce them, but actually believe in the person I was and the talents I had, is something incredible. It was because of you that I know a lot more about the person I am, and there is nothing that can change that.

Not only do I owe you so much, but so many people do as well. You are the epitome of goodness in this world, while being a pillar in the truest sense possible. I could not be prouder of you and your life ethics. I may not always agree with you, though I know who you are above all. A wife, mother, inspiration and pillar. The rest is irrelevant, as long as we can look out for each other.

Furthermore, I know I am not the only one to believe these things about you. May you one day see yourself as we all do. Don't worry, most people live to see themselves in a future where their past doesn't matter. At that point, what matters is to pass down that knowledge to our children so they can have a better life than we ever dreamed of having.

I'm not worried about our past or future. All I am worried about is making sure we both keep a sane outlook in life. As long as we keep having the discussions we have, I'm positive we'll both gain wisdom together. Over time, we'll inspire each other to become better for our own sanity.

Visionary

Living a life is to know who we are becoming, day by day from the moment we see the world

The envisioned future is one where the betterment of our crafts and lives become a statement, as opposed to a mere vision. That said, the visionary in you speaks volumes about what you want and what you seek in life. As you perceive the future, you see one full of greatness for both yourself and I.

It may not always be evident to create that future, as we can only control what we can. Still, that way you have of wanting something or envisioning it, is never easy to do. Yet, you do it day in and day out. Zeinab, the world is your oyster that you can carve out. Every step of the way, you have thus far been able to become better through what you wanted seen accomplished.

True, we all have a vision of sorts. Or at the very least, a dream we want for ourselves. But the truth is that most people don't have that determination to see it through. Instead of reaching for the stars, they simply dream a dream - no real vision to speak of. As for you, you don't even know the definition of that. You trudge through life, with your abilities spearheading all of those initiatives.

At the end of the rainbow is the sought-out finish line. Whether it takes a year or a decade, you've never given up. You've cried, struggled, and questioned the very core of the being that you were. At the end, you've gotten back up every single time, since you refuse to give up or give into the temptation that leads to utter despair.

The person who has a vision and is steadfast wants to see it through. As far as I am aware, the vision you have is to help create a better world for those who struggle with themselves. It is hard to see the potential, the greatness and talent in ourselves. Most of us will never see those emerge out of us, because we don't know how to see what you see. You elevate others, because your vision is one that allows you to create those opportunities for them.

The difficulty in that is so astronomical. On the other hand, you have an amazing talent that most people would love possessing. To be so astute and perceptive in a world that mostly knows chaos is a true gift. I wish the world could see that gift that you have. Even when you are different at times from others on so many levels, it never matters. You have a knack to be someone everyone wants to be underneath the surface.

To have that confidence within yourself, others can only wish to have that. Yet, the image you envision for them is that same confidence, but one buried deep down beneath the surface of their being. You're capable of helping them retrieve it, because you want everyone to have that same opportunity that others have.

When people are so different from each other, it can be so painful to see them fail when they are trying to reach for the stars. When they are unable to do so, you have the ability to reach your hand out, so as to help them back up. The vision someone else has doesn't have to go to the wayside. As you help them up, you're capable of doing so because no one truly reaches their potential without help.

If anything, you're the reason I've succeeded on so many levels, even though sometimes it doesn't feel that way. I've accomplished so much because you were there to guide me. If not for you, I wouldn't have published several books already, nor would I have had a fairly good paying job as my first true professional job. Nor would I have understood that so many difficulties in my life were derived from having Asperger's. So much has made sense because of you.

Your ability to push through is a rare one. I'm so proud of you, as I've seen others do and accomplish great things because of you. This speaks volumes about the person you are and have become. Not only are you great at what you do, but you've never settled for anything less than what you deserve. I think the reason for that is when you were younger, you probably thought you'd have to settle for someone and settle for a mediocre job and so on. Instead, you've persevered and pushed through a world that often doesn't know what is truly good on this earth.

I may not always give myself enough credit for what I've accomplished on this earth, but I do know one thing for certain: I will not rest until you give yourself all the credit that you deserve. To do what you do and be who you are - despite so many obstacles - is quite a feat on its own. To be a black woman in a white world (well in North America anyhow) is extremely challenging. I may never know what that feels like or looks like at the moment for you in any given situation, but I know that you are a fighter. I've never seen you give up, regardless of the odds or the stakes at play.

All those times I've seen you wipe tears from your face, not once have you stayed defeated. Rather, you took it as an opportunity to learn and become better because of it. That's part of what makes that person inside you become greater. I may not see a world full of potential or beauty, but you've always been willing to be that person that is unwilling to give up on the world.

Often, people never see what I do or how good I am at it. It reminds me of one my all-time favourite shows called Monk. You're the one person that refuses to not see the beginning of my potential. That unwillingness to turn a blind eye to my creativity is something no one else could ever do. Because you are the Trudy to my Monk. Your sincere ability to devote yourself to acknowledge someone else's potential is not something I've ever seen before.

My English teacher (Barry O'Connell) believed in my writing skills and he's the reason I've been writing for twenty plus years. Aside from him, I wish there would have been other people in between him and you that would have seen that same potential (and some more). If not for you, I'm not sure where I would be or what I would do. In any event, thank you for being the person I needed to have in my life.

That goal in life everyone wants to aspire to is never as far as we think. Sure, it is to a certain degree and can be daunting at times. Yet, the road to Rome begins by laying down a single brick at a time. And before you know it, you'll reach the end of the road in no time! Ok, that's a lie. It takes time and isn't always a smooth ride, although it's worth it once you realize you're at the end of it.

The problem is that most people think that success is accomplished within five minutes. It can, but it usually isn't. Which is why when I see you accomplish with others what they fail to accomplish by themselves, it's good to know that I have you in my corner. You truly have a unique gift when it comes to having a vision set for yourself or others. When I see you do mundane things that I myself dread doing, it reminds me how much you push yourself to do the easy and hard things all at once.

Perhaps one day, the world will see what you're capable of doing, as I know for a fact that what seems easy is often pretty hard to accomplish. That being said, you can't accomplish anything if you do nothing about it. Whatever happens, just keep pushing and one day you'll see all your efforts rewarded. It may not be someone who sees what you're doing, but Allah as He rewards all your efforts in this world.

In any event, never give up when it seems everything is fading into obscurity. Where is darkness, there is always a hint of light that shines through. Be it through the window, beneath the door or even a glimmer from the moon itself. I know you wouldn't give up, but it's always nice having someone reminding you you're not alone. Moreover, the affirmation that there is at least another person that believes in you is monumental in your journey.

It may even seem like the journey is long if not almost everlasting, but that's only because humans experience a lifespan considerably longer than anything else on earth. For the little time we have here on this planet, always remember that what you want for yourself and others is not impossible and can be accomplished. I am aware I often don't feel that way, although I know you'll always be there to remind me. If anything, I'll be there to remind you as well.

Whatever anyone may say, never give in to that darkness, and always be proud of the person you are. Few people can claim they have such a grasp on life the same way you do. They'll often struggle to find themselves, as they lose part of their being. Remember that the talent and potential that resides in others also resides within.

No one can take away the greatness in you, regardless of what they try to do. Keep reaching for the stars, and never lose sight of yourself in the process. If you need me, I'll be there to support you on your journey.

Beyond A Simple Wife

Measuring the good and the bad only raises questions about who we are, and who we could be

To me, you will always be more than a simple wife. For all the things I've seen you do, you are a lot more than how I could ever see you. Day and night, you always watch out for both of us. I know I try and fail, while you're always a step ahead. I can't thank you enough for everything that you do, day in and day out.

Perhaps that is the biggest difference between men and women. The ability of women to care for others is more natural, as only you have the ability to physically carry a child in your womb. Because of that, you are inclined to worry about your husband as well.

This natural talent is part of what makes women the pillar of the family, as they are typically seen as the protector of the household. Sure, men are usually stronger when it comes to physically protecting their family. But it is women who tend to be there to make sure their children and husbands are safe. You have a strength within you that permits you to be an integral part of the household.

I fully know you want me to be there more in certain aspects, but what you do and how you do it is certainly something that you're a lot more capable of than me. There is something in your personality as well that strengthens your resolve. Trust me, I am fully aware that you want me to be strong too. I may never be as strong as you, but I've gotten a lot better. There is less fear in my eyes, despite some struggles that I've had to deal with.

Like a lot of women, you are a super woman. Half of the things you do around the house, I struggle with. As for what you do for your own sake to better yourself, I struggle to be as resilient. If anything, you've accomplished so much for yourself. Not only that, you've also done so much to help me on my journey. As the saying goes, "behind every great man is a great woman". Having undertaken the tasks you have during your journey is truly something.

Be proud of yourself and who you are becoming. I will always appreciate the way you watch out for others, despite the fact that no one says you ever had to. Be it me or complete strangers that you don't even know. You're always willing to give the benefit of the doubt to people you've never even met.

My brother might have literally climbed Mount Kilimanjaro years ago, but you've figuratively climbed Mount Everest. That tenacity is incredible to say the least. You are more than a simple wife, you are the most amazing woman I've ever seen in my life. After all, I could only dedicate those words to the singular person that has [more than] attempted knowing the person I am.

It takes patience and love to be consistently surrounded by a ball of energy. Yet, you persevere and learn to be more than simply Zeinab. On my side, I would lie if I said it's always easy, but I've learned to be better for you. At least, I think so. It may not always show that I ameliorate myself for you, but I do. Perhaps the steps are not as big as you'd want them to be, but I try.

As I said, you are more than a wife. Every time I think about what you do, and how much you do, I am always surprised at the energy you somehow find as you do those things. You certainly deserve more credit than you give yourself, and perhaps more than I give you as well. Nonetheless, I know the depth of what you accomplish both at home and at work.

The composure you have when it comes to situations - be they hard or easy - is astounding. True, you do cry once in a while because life can be hard on us at times. Which is why I try my best to listen to what's on your mind. It's also true I don't always find it easy to fully pay attention, as it does tend to overwhelm me.

Beyond all of this, I can't imagine my life without you. Not for the things you do, rather for the strength you have within you. There are times that you wanted to give up, yet you chose to wipe your tears away and overcome any obstacles in your path. I not only appreciate that about you, but also the unyielding courage in the person you are.

Within a world that isn't always kind, your soul is strong. Those times you're having issues dealing with it, I'll always be a pillar you can lean on. I know it won't always seem like it if at all, yet I'll always do the best that I can. I realize that my best won't always be what it should be. For that, I apologize.

I hope you can forgive those times that I am not the person I should be. There are times where the world gets to me as well, but I'll do my best, nonetheless. As the earth shatters and crumbles beneath our feet, we can be there for each other. We can be each other's soulful strength, as we find solace in knowing that life is but a steppingstone in this journey.

Still, you are a lot more than my wife. You are the Sixth Pillar in Islam. Of that, I can only be proud to share this journey with you. As you're well aware, it was never easy and never will be. That's why we have each other, so we can support one another throughout these long years ahead of us. Whether we live an extra fifty or eighty years, there will always be times of hardships. To be fair, we've experienced most of those already. Perhaps what we can look forward to are years of happiness without any true sadness.

Whatever happens, know that you represent more than you could ever imagine to others and myself. Words will never tell you how much you mean to me. If anything, I could never express myself well enough when it comes to you. All I know, is that you've brought so much into my life in such a way that I am thankful for.

Despite all the fears you may have, always remember that every single thing that you do is never overlooked, ignored or unappreciated. I wish I had your resilience in all things, because I've never seen anyone else be the way they are. Not only that, but the way you help elevate me in what I do, thank you.

Furthermore, being the woman you are is a Godsend. I couldn't imagine you being different than who and what you are. Continue to be that singular individual, as only you can be that person.

The biggest irony in all my life was that I wasn't looking for you, but somehow you found me. If not for you, who knows where I would be. In all of this, you became better for it and learned so much from me, as my love was always unconditional. This was something you've always appreciated to this day.

We have both been humbled by each other in terms of allowing the betterment of the other. We've certainly learnt a lot, which is how and why we'll continue on being the better half of each other.

When complications arise, it's easier to leave everything behind instead of working at it. The truth of the matter, when something becomes hard or complicated, we've sometimes felt troubled by the situation. However, the only way to have a long-lasting relationship is to work at it. I'm confident we've always done that.

Truly, it takes a lot of effort, dedication, empathy and so much more to be that resilient. The idea of living with one person for an entire lifespan is certainly remarkable. When I saw my grandparents together till the end, I couldn't have imagined anything else.

Despite a society that would believe relationships are often limited or potentially doomed to failure, there are always solutions to any problem.

To have seen you be willing thus far to make sure [with me] that we got to work through any issues we may have had, it takes a very special person to acknowledge that love finds a way. There may come a time where things occur, but I'm confident that we'll always find a solution to anything.

In all earnestness, there isn't anyone else that compares to the person you are. I know I should probably say it more, although I am sure you think I already do. Thank you for being the woman I've always known you to be.

Understanding And Brave

Walking towards a finish line, without knowing the outcome or even the journey can be difficult

One of the qualities which is hard to come by is the one of understanding. Being capable of accepting people, as well as giving them the benefit of the doubt is not something that's easy to do. Somehow, you manage to do just that.

There is bravery in trusting the world to be what it often is not. Somehow, you're able to be that ray of hope in a world often shrouded in darkness. Despite believing certain things, you still won't judge others because you don't agree with them.

To be this way is both rare and unexpected. I may be easily annoyed or frustrated like many others, yet you seem to find light where the rest of us only see darkness. There is something within you that allows you to be a greater individual on so many levels. The more you understand others, the more knowledge you gain.

The ability to see why someone does something very specific is a skill hard to come by. I've never met anyone who was willing to look at themselves the way you do and consider what your words and actions mean to that other person.

You can singlehandedly help others or make them feel welcomed. Perhaps being different in so many ways from a lot of people here forced you to see individuals not through their words, but through their actions. In this, there is true bravery. Allowing yourself to understand people through this is commendable.

Even though Oprah was the first black woman that was heard on an impactful level in our era, I can only imagine that one day you could become the next voice after Oprah and Michelle Obama (and others I am unaware of).

For the last twenty plus years, we've seen a lot of things that made people question their own humanity. Like you, others have had to voice themselves to be heard. Sometimes, for the sake of understanding, and other times for displaying a broken system.

Since the events set in motion by 9/11, as well as by Colin Kaepernick by taking a knee and looking more closely as to why First Nations women went missing, a lot more attention has been placed on discrimination. The question in any of these scenarios was: Why is this happening?

The reality is that it's easy to ignore words, as they seldom affect the person speaking them in the first place. Consider this: The words of Martin Luther King Jr. would have a greater impact on those who would seek to silence him. The knee taken by Colin Kaepernick placed a greater emphasis on those who sought to silence him, just as much as the discussions surrounding missing First Nation women here in Canada.

For years, it was easier to ignore our own misunderstanding, ignorance and/or arrogance. It's easy to see why the term "white [male] privilege" is something that only recently became a more known term in North America. Furthermore, with the voices in entertainment rising such as Colin Kaepernick's, LeBron James', and P.K. Subban's among others, it's harder to ignore what they saw growing up or might even still be experiencing.

For those people sharing their voices - regardless of income - it has created a movement over the years. Not only for Black Lives Matter, but one which is starting to affect something greater as a whole. Hence the new remake of the Wonder Years featuring an all black cast, among other things such as the phrases basketball and football players wear. This, among other initiatives, is to give a voice to people who seldom had one in the past.

These voices validate that there was never anything wrong with you, but rather with those who sought to silence you. Perhaps this is why you are hard on yourself. I've mostly lived what you would call a normal life, and I can't imagine what it meant for you to be that one different person growing up. I just hope that everything you've experienced in life can heal over time.

I can't speak for others, but I personally never cared what people looked like. That is what Islam teaches. As I wrote in my autobiography, "[w]ho am I to be anything but the colour of Islam?" The "colour of Islam" contains everyone. We may be different on the surface, but underneath our cultures and preferences, we all stand up, sit, eat and sleep the same.

We all belong on earth as equals, despite the fact that this is sadly not always the case. To quote myself again, "I belong to one race: the human race." Most people forget that, and use the word "race" to speak about a very superficial aspect of their being. The colour of my skin is merely due to a lack of sunlight in a Nordic country. It means nothing else. The fact that is does to so many people is disheartening.

Beyond these discussions, you've looked past people and tried understanding who they are. Doing that is not so obvious, as we often use our culture to create a bubble, which in turn makes us believe we are "righter" than someone else. The fact that you're looking past that is admirable. A lot of people are unable to do this.

You've certainly helped me see the world even more widely now. I hope that one day others will see the world as you see it, and be less judgemental.

In one of our conversations if I recall correctly, you mentioned an interesting verse from a Hadith that states that the end of days will be near when we won't be able to tell the difference between men and women. This, ironically, could be also be interpreted as people being unable to judge others on how they look as well. After all, if you can't tell who is who, you'd either judge no one or end up judging everyone (and probably get tired of doing so after a while).

I realize it's difficult for the entire human race to be righteous. Still, the way we treat others has a true impact on them and who we perceive them to be. If Mother Theresa was more than willing to work with individuals with leprosy, then how can it be so hard to treat each other in a civil and humane way? Most of us fail to be a fraction of who she was. She worked with people others deemed as mortal walking diseases.

The reality is that it takes a truly understanding and brave woman to acknowledge everything about herself and others. Despite the fact that both of us could be better, like Mother Theresa or Martin Luther King Jr., we can still be at the very least a fraction of what they were. Most importantly, to be as transparent as they were when it came to their humanity.

There was nothing hidden away or uncertain about either, they were who they were without an ounce of superficiality. Both risked their lives doing what they did, yet they couldn't have imagined being someone they were not. To me, you are partly like them. At least, you are a voice they could never be in their era. Neither had social media, the internet nor a marvel of technology. However, they rose to become legends in their own right.

With all of this technology at your disposal, I know you've already made an impact by helping others. Once you realize they can attain their potential, you see how grateful they are as they accomplish great things because of your support. I will try my best to support you, so you don't have to feel alone.

As for me, I try to have more courage as a person. I wish I had that same determination I see in you. We may have both experienced trauma when we were younger, but it was because of you that I started releasing it (well, some of it). Whatever trauma that you might still be experiencing, remember the youth of your parents and your grandparents.

For every tear, just remember your parents most likely had doubled those tears, while your grandparents had four times that amount. If anything, I know it's because of the generational trauma that you wanted to be stronger for others. When someone cannot express themselves or fight for themselves, they need a voice.

As far as I know, you've become to be that singular voice for others by helping them. I'm sure they're all very grateful as well for what you've accomplished on their behalf. It's hard to be voiceless, as others won't try to understand them, as it's easier to judge that person for what they're not saying because they're incapable of doing so.

I know for a fact that you've done so much for others in that regard. Possessing the ability to comprehend unspoken words is a gift. Wherever you get in life, don't ever forget who you are, and what you mean to people.

Individuals who know the person you are remembers the brave soul within you. As tears may fall upon your cheeks, don't forget that we are all in the same boat. It's just that a lot don't know it yet.

Kindhearted Beyond Belief

To weave a tapestry with only good words only brings out the best in you

What I appreciate most about you is that you're always willing to admit you're wrong when you are. Also, you have a very caring heart. Initially when we met, you decided to give me another chance, as you weren't sure about me. You could have easily been on your merry way and never looked back.

If anything, you only saw a generic person at first. Almost void of a true personality and empathetic nature, despite neither of us knowing I had Asperger's at the time. Which probably didn't allow you to see the person I truly was. I tend to appear fairly bland when faced with people I don't know much about, if anything. At least, I think so. I could be wrong, as I've never found myself to be with myself in that regard (assuming this makes sense).

Instead of looking away, you opted to see if more could be unearthed beneath the surface of the person I portrayed myself as. Upon doing so, you discovered a wealth of emotions that flowed through the art of writing. Mostly letters (if not all) that I had written years before. You saw someone that existed on a different level of existence. You were inspired to witness the rise of something special within someone.

I think that is what made you start understanding that the adage was true about not judging a book by its cover. There is always more beneath what we outwardly see when looking at someone else. Perhaps due to this, you became more kindhearted as a person. You grasped the notion that we are who we are, but not only the surface.

In fact, I recall when we had gone to a BBQ in Atlanta when we flew there. I can't remember the person's name (as I don't know who he was specifically), but he invited two young children aged around ten or so on stage, in front of the crowd. Then, he offered the first boy the possibility to choose between two things. The first was outright money (probably around $5), while the second thing was just a crumpled-up Kleenex or paper towel. He picked the money, and so he gave the crumpled-up tissue to the other boy. Then, he asked the boy to open it. Inside, there was $20.

That was a lesson in both humility and to not judge someone (or something) based on outward appearances. Be it because of how they communicate, the colour of their skin or what their names are.

It may be true that I am the peanut gallery as you so love to call me, but I do listen to the important stuff. You've certainly helped both of us to have a greater understanding when it comes to being fairer to others, as we can't truly know what's inside without really knowing.

At the end of the day, what becomes twice as important is the fact that you've grown to not only be brave, but also kindhearted. I think the older we get, the less we want to deal with utter nonsense. For some of us, like yourself, this means ignoring negativity as much as possible while focusing on the positive. It's not always easy to say the least, but I know you try your hardest to be better for yourself.

Beyond the simple journey you probably set out for yourself initially, you learnt more about the world that surrounds us as you started becoming older. Once we reach our teens and early twenties, we experience the world in a selfish way for the most part. Once you reach your thirties and up, that's when you realize that life isn't what you expected it to be, both physically and mentally.

On a physical level, it gets harder as we can develop arthritis, or other serious problems with our health. While the mental aspect of it becomes different, as anguish is different. It's not as intense as those bouts of profound emotional strife as when we were eighteen. But the pain still exists, while we possess a deeper understanding that the mortal self is finite. With youth comes a sense of infinity.

Perhaps this is the reason you became a more caring individual. On the other hand, we still need to work on that for your own self. But for now, however, learn to appreciate that same beauty that others see within you.

There is a singular thing I've noticed with you over the years since we've been married, which is your ability to see the rights and the wrongs that you yourself fall prey to at times. To acknowledge our faults is never easy, yet your capacity for finding that rare strength within you to see past a selfish self is admirable.

Truthfully, you've become a paragon of kindness for others to look at. You may never see yourself as so, as you've often been very hard on yourself to even realize the beauty within. There is a reason why people such as Brené Brown and Gary Vaynerchuk exist.

They were created to help people see past a shallowed self as to be better for our self, just as the baker exists to facilitate us to buy a delicious (albeit extremely unhealthy) cake that we may not have the time to bake, or that we may simply end up burning in the oven. To pretend we know something outside of our craft would be very foolish indeed.

At the end of the road, you've still come a long way. We both have, as we're still growing. Sure, the physical body mostly stops growing at twenty-five (except cartilage), but our actual mental growth never ceases to exist. The more our lives go on, the more we discover a bit about ourselves.

Just as you've seen growth in me, I've witnessed a lot in you as well. I don't know if you've realized it or seen it, but it's there. Hopefully you can branch off of that progress you've made to become a better person for the world, to be a better one for yourself.

Yes, I do think you have become more kindhearted over time as you've had to grow up like I have. We've experienced so much together, probably a lot more than many others may have. Regardless of any situation we've been in, we've been forced to see our lives in a different light every single time when something happened. If anything, I'm glad that we've had those experiences, not out of joy or happiness, but because we'll be able to use those experiences as both teaching tools and building blocks.

What better way is there to help others or your own children when you've experienced devastating losses? Those may not prepare us to be the people we would have wanted to be twenty years ago, but they'll certainly help us to help others. Or perhaps to help us be more resilient should those things happen again.

The funny thing about life is that you keep on learning things, as well as simply growing up. I assume that we'll both settle in our ways in our older age, but for now, perhaps we could learn more about the world. The ease of life, as well as the void which torments us is but a passage in time. It may not be pleasant, although we all experience pain, disappointment and so much more like everyone else.

Perhaps our pain is different, just as much as how we grew up and where we grew up. Our experiences were certainly different. If there was one thing that changed you throughout time was your kindness, as you've only wanted others to accept you. But for that, you need to accept yourself, so that others are either forced to do the same or simply outright ignore you.

I know you place a lot of strain on yourself at times, as you would like for the world to see itself as you want to see it. To give a chance to others when others do not always give you that chance can truly feel harrowing at times. Know this: Despite what the world gives out, just remember there are always good people out there who believe what you believe in.

If they were ever to meet you, they would tell you that you've got a good heart, and that it can be difficult at times to not receive that same energy you put out into the world.

If there is anything, I will always remember when you told me about a time when you were just a child. You told me that another girl didn't want to play with you because you were black. I can't imagine what that felt like, as that's never been something I had to worry about. I'm so sorry you had to go through such an ordeal at a young age.

I don't know what I would say to any of our children if they had to experience that. Knowing me, you know I would most likely tell them the harsh realities of this world. Not to frighten them, but to help them be as resilient as I would have liked to have been growing up. I'd want them to have as many tools at their disposal as possible. Resilience, at least for me, is something I envy in others. If my children could possess a single emotional tool, I'd want them to have that within them.

For me, resilience is something I truly wish I had throughout my life. After all, one of those things we want our children to have are things we couldn't have or simply didn't have growing up. If our children could be resilient instead of enduring psychological trauma, they could become a stronger version of us.

That being said, I'm glad that your experiences have not made you bitter or angry because of multiple incidents in your past. At this point in your life, I think you've done a lot better than you might have expected years ago. In other ways, a lot better than I ever have. It's true that I have a real strength when it comes to not overly caring about much because of how my brain works due to my Asperger's, but you're getting there as well. The difference is that you've had to actually work at it.

Pious While Feeling Impious

Realizing both success and failures are part of life, we can only dream of having positive results

Perhaps not as strangely as I would have imagined, you have a sense of pride when it comes to certain things in relation to Islam. It certainly took you a while to get where you were, but you got there. I suppose it's hard to determine what piety even truly means.

I do recall when you told me, around ten years ago, that even when I was practising Islam when I didn't really know much, that if I could try to be better despite my very limited knowledge, then you should be able to improve. You said it inspired you to become a better person for yourself.

If anything, one of my favourite quotes comes from a song from the Spice Girls, which ironically, you'd think their songs would be all sparkly because of how they sang and their bubbly personalities. Yet, deep lyrics were hidden if you listened for them. One of their songs called "Wannabe" says, "If you want my future, forget my past". That could mean something extremely superficial, just as much as something dark and sinister. But, the point is simply to not hold anything against that person when it comes to errors in judgement, or lack of faith or conviction among a myriad of things.

The more we hold onto negative emotions or behaviours, the more it's likely to hurt one or both individuals. The ability to learn, forgive or forget, can be a very critical component in reaching a higher level of humanity. As in our personal growth. Through time, pain, scars and healing form a part of the person we are. When we learn to forgive mistakes of any sort, that is when we can be a more balanced self. To hold onto negative emotions is in and of itself negative.

Regardless, we all bear the scars from our childhood, teenagerhood, young adulthood and even the present day. Through time, we try to harness positivity to become a ray of hope, so that we can be that person that someone else needs.

Being good or bad is not pious or impious in and of itself, simply because not all acts are weighed the same. The most important part in this case is to remember to be positive towards our own selves. After all, we are our biggest enemy. We fail because we are afraid of being successful, as much as we are afraid of how others perceive us. Trust me, I know.

The more we want to be pious in this life, the more we fail. Not because of our inability to be so, but rather due to the fact that we don't want to give up. As such, we fail just as much. It certainly is hard, as we want to avoid that sense of dread.

The truth is, we all hold emotional baggage that forces us to be the person we are. That doesn't mean we become the person we want to be. Having the inexperience in this life that we've had thus far, made us question how to live life in the process. That being said, the older we got as we subsequently reached our thirties, that's when we began having a better yet bleaker understanding of life.

While generations change in terms of the technology we grow up in, or how people behave or what type of music we listen to, it becomes part of our trauma and disbelief. When we were children, I remember that my grandmother's house door was never locked. Now, it is.

We trusted our neighbours, and actually spent time with them. In our case, we had at least four or five neighbours (or technically households) that we either invited over or went over to their place.

I remember when I was maybe ten or twelve years old, I had a neighbour in his late twenties or early thirties. He lived with his mother, and had a motorcycle. He had offered for me to ride with him at some point.

Back then, you would have thought nothing of such a thing, but times change where we would think the worst of that person. Believing that he would have ulterior motives (he did NOT, he was just a nice neighbour), people now would believe the worst of those types of situations.

The way times change is traumatic to a certain degree, as we saw our youth being much safer because we had trust. Something we do not have any longer. Of all this to say that despite our insecurities about how we lived life, we have to remember that all those traumatic thoughts and experiences were created during a huge traumatic experience which was our transition from what we considered a safer world into one which we don't always understand. At the end of the day, our nieces and nephews probably have no idea why we say "tape" instead of "record", nor would they know what a VCR or a VHS Tape is among other things. Not only that, but they probably can't conceive how we ever used [paper] maps, assuming they even heard of a [paper] map.

All of these events, behaviours and ways of thinking led you and I to question the person we were along the way in our journey. So, any notions we had when it came to being inadequate or even Haram (forbidden), it's because we are human. After all, to err is human.

The funny part about humanity is that we "only" live to be maybe a hundred. Key word, maybe. A hundred years seems like forever until you realize the mortality within time itself. It was just yesterday that I was fifteen years old and playing Role Playing Games (RPGs), or so it feels like it. At the end of it all, a large part of what we do is Halal (permissible) or Haram.

If truth be told, none of us is entering paradise, as every single one of us has done Haram things. Again, to be human is to be imperfect. Which is why we seek forgiveness and guidance, despite our inability to be that Halal person we'd all want to be. In His mercy and wisdom, He can forgive us as a parent looks at their kid full of blueberries on their face, as we ask them if they ate the pie. The child lies, but the parent knows the truth. We don't forsake the young one for lying, as the nature of a child is to be a child. Just as much as to be human is to be imperfect. Most importantly, in the eyes of an infinite God, we are but mere children.

Whatever we do, we can only ask for forgiveness, and find solutions to become better. I don't know how I've become a more pious individual if at all, although I know that I try my best. You do as well, and if there is any lesson for us to see would be the following: Never lose hope in who we are, because no one else can make us be who we are.

We've come a long way from the children, teenagers and young adults that we once were, as we now have much more experiences under our belt. Imagine that? Still, we are defined by those experiences, as well as any shame we feel. In any event, just remember we can't all recite the Qur'an by heart, be phenomenal physicists or be incredibly gifted in sports. I'm... still waiting for you to master a couple of videogames.

Beneath the grim reality of life at times, we all feel pious and impious. It's part of being extremely complex beings. Don't judge yourself too harshly during those moments that hold you back, as there are many more moments where you can feel good about what you do, and who you are.

It's ok to feel great, as it is to have no sense of direction. I may not have really seen your growth spiritually, as we lived individual lives for almost thirty years before we met. What I do know are those times that you pray - while performing your duties as a Muslim in a serious manner - that we can do better, even when that's only an inch at a time.
When I see you like that, it reminds me that we're not perfect (hence our prayers). It certainly isn't easy to remember this, since we often forget to

forgive ourselves while feeling afraid that we're not doing the best that we possibly can.

It's in those moments that we can become better for ourselves, and be level-headed. Otherwise, we risk seeing a part of the world and ourselves as something it's really not. The peace that you've found over the years is a fraction of the one you'll hope to find throughout decades to come.

Socially Kind

Within the grasp of a world so finite, sometimes the only way to live is altruistically

In spite of a troubled life, which we have all suffered through, you still learnt to be kind. Whereas it's effortless for any of us to speak our minds, or get angry. It takes no energy to be that type of person, yet it takes a lot to be someone who pours their heart out to others in such a way that enables you to remind them of their humanity. Most importantly, of the strength within them, even when they fail to realize they have potential.

There are other times when you want to help people for the sake of aiding them, as being in a disadvantaged position is never easy. It brings individuals into a stressful and anxious situation, which can become disheartening. You might not know if they are in dire need of help, or if they're being dishonest at the moment.

You rather trust that someone be honest, and help them if you think they genuinely need help. Should they be dishonest with you, shame on them. Allah is always watching and knows. Being deceitful once is one thing, but being so continuously is as bad as negative energy.

Perhaps we've walked a different path in our educational years, but I think the most impactful events that shaped who we became were related to people close to us. Be they related to abandonment, neglect, or other traumas. Be they parents, siblings or friends, we've all been touched by situations that had a great impact on us.

Then, there are other events that you witness happening to others, or even to yourself. That's when you realize that the world can either be the same or at times worse than what you've experienced in life thus far.

I've seen situations and people that were disappointing. I've seen several cons in Montreal at the metro stations and other places. I remember this one lady asking money for the metro fare. Afterwards, she would keep doing the same thing. I was waiting for my friend, and noticed she kept doing that for the entire fifteen minutes I was there. At that point, that's outright theft in my opinion. But, for all I know, she might not have been in her right mind. I've seen some quite erratic behaviour, from someone sticking their tongue out at me, to people outright talking to themselves.

There was another time where a man had a stomach deformity (although it could have been due to insulin injections - not sure). He approached me and the person I was with, asking for forty dollars for a taxi. He said he had to go to the hospital for something, maybe some tests I assume.

He said he would have his lawyer send us the money. When he said that, it made no sense to me then, and it still makes no sense to me now. I never carry money anyhow for security reasons. Eventually, I saw him months later telling the exact same story to a couple at a metro station.

When you witness things of that nature, how can we trust people? The amount of times I've been lied to makes me not trust others. On the other hand, you have a more trusting nature, as you rather forgive once, with the "shame on them" mentality if they lied to you.

I can't say what's a better approach to being socially kind. It's a strength that I lack, since it's hard for me to give the same trust you openly give others. That being said, even when a part of me wants you to be more suspicious of people, I can't realistically expect you to be someone you're not. All I can hope for is that nothing bad happens, and that you're safe regardless of the outcome of the situation.

Believe it or not, despite the goodwill in our desire for the world to be better in the generation we live in, most of our time is spent being distrustful of others. I can't pretend to know why things have changed over the course of the last twenty years, but something has. Regardless, I don't think your outlook has changed. What I do know is that the kindness you show the world won't be changing any time soon.

Perhaps the changes are due to the evolution of humankind in terms of our intellectual prowess, as much as our dedication to creating a better life for ourselves and others. That does, however, bring just as much problems as solutions. Whatever we solved, we created newer issues. Mostly social ones. This brings us to a gap between two distinct generations.

Our memories of the eighties and nineties are tainted with a lens that newer generations will never understand. Moving about in the world, whether virtually or physically was completely different back then compared to now. As time moved on, we saw the emergence of differences coming about when we saw the rise of modern technology, AI (as in actual human like behaviour), as well as the advancement within the realm of transportation.

When you add all of these together, we saw the changes appear in a subtle way, where trust in humanity was lost one bit at a time. It became easier to trust a machine rather than a person. A machine can't lie. The worst it can do is tell you something inaccurate, as it was programmed incorrectly to begin with. Although, it's true that there are some people who would rather be dishonest on purpose because it's easy for them to get away with it.

Whereas the AI is shackled to be limited, as initially pondered by Isaac Asimov, often known as the three laws of Asimov. I've seen several actual AIs that look human as well. Not only that, but Saudi Arabia granted citizenship to an actual almost lifelike AI. The fact that some people would even consider AI to be sentient is problematic to say the least, as they are mere robotic creations. I will always be haunted by the line from Mass Effect 3 from a robot known as a Geth, "[d]o these units have a soul?"

Since the world is heading in that direction, we've lost sight of the humanity within us. The outcome or rather consequence of that is that we have a greater fear of our fellow human, as AIs don't lie. At least not yet.

Nonetheless, you still have faith in the world, hoping that any pain is genuine and sincere. While we step out into the real world, there is a magnitude of a difference compared to the semi-virtual world that was created with the advent of the internet and other modern technologies.

There are times where I see humans living in a world that they don't understand, where developments happen for the best (mostly), without the knowledge behind it. From when penicillin was first discovered by a Scottish physician, or when virtual reality or even mixed reality became something normal. It feels like we are children that have toys, but don't know how they're made, nor do we question how they function.

Due to that, we've lost sight of what it means to be human. The human connection is not a reality any longer as it once was. Now, we have family, friends and internet friends, fleet mates, guild members and clansmen (am I missing any?). We've diluted what real interaction was before.

Somehow, you manage to strip the virtual aspect, and just use the social kindness within you. Whether in person or not, you always want to depict yourself as being who you are. You see no point in any form of deception.

There is a reason why people go to you. Sure, they go to you because you're good at what you do, but most importantly, you're good at being you. To still be the person underneath both reality and virtuality, is a feat in and of itself. It's so rare to be that same individual day in and day out, without at least being a little deceptive.

You've never lost that essence in you. If anything, you became more genuine over time and became kinder on a social level. People have no idea of all that, but I do know they appreciate this about you, even thought they have no clue.

What I can say is that you should remind yourself of the efforts you've made. Not only for others, but for your family and yourself. To be a compassionate individual takes a lot of energy, yet it seems that you have the ability to be just that. Never let anyone else dictate to you what you can and cannot do.

There is a strength in you that I wish I had. To have that confidence in yourself that you do, as much as both the inward and outward appearance that you have (i.e. how you present yourself), would be phenomenal to possess those qualities. It's not to say I don't have my own.

More Human Than The Average

Outside the confines of the person we think we are, lies greater possibilities for us as humans

To engage with someone can be hard, frustrating, and even outright annoying. I personally don't have the patience to be that way on a consistent level. I have if I had to, but it was never easy being placed in those situations.

Somehow, you have an energy within you. You've always been willing to interact with others, while actively making sure that their voices are heard when they speak to you. Not only that, but you go beyond merely speaking with them. And yes, despite the fact that you are a know-it-all, you have a good heart.

To actively engage with others means to be willing to be there for them. Due to this, there is something about you that makes you more human than most. If you consider how we are as a society, some of the saddest depictions of our communities include: Our distrust of others, our inability to forgive, as well as our unwillingness to help others. Most importantly, the reticence we have to treat everyone equally as first-class citizens.

It's very easy to place zero faith in others, as it doesn't cost us anything monetarily speaking or risk wise. Therefore, within humanity itself on a global basis, there are so many examples of us failing as humans. Less than half the eligible population goes out to vote, while other people are throwing racial slurs at athletes because of their origins, while there are also others who think it is their God given right to tell individuals their religion is oppressive.

This is the state of the world we live in, not to mention other events we may not see, while they still occur on a daily basis. Whether a situation could be seen as good or bad, we're often unaware of the fact that they're taking place. That by itself is mind-blowing, considering the access traditional media has in our society.

To see past what the Shaytan wants us to see, somehow there's a lot we manage to not see. He makes us blind to the light at the end of the tunnel, trying to perpetually keep us inside it, where there's only darkness abound.

There is goodness in each of us if we're willing to take an honest peek inside ourselves. Be it to create a better life for ourselves or to make sure that others have a better chance of surviving this oft cruel world.

I can't speak for the rest of the world, as they're literally an ocean away, but for what it's worth, I know that our democracy was never meant to protect the majority of the population. There's no point in trying to protect the majority of the people, when their way of life is guaranteed. Instead, it's about protecting those whose inability to be heard can be heeded through an advocate on their behalf.

Having someone in your corner when your voice seems meaningless is a great tool. After all, you may not be a lawyer, a barrister or even a paralegal, although I've seen you advocate for others. Even though I wish for those with power would do so, it has to start somewhere. Usually, this begins at the grassroots level.

Your willingness to listen and make sure someone is treated fairly is quite uncommon in the grander scheme of things. When someone is on the brink of either giving up, or has already lost faith in themselves, I've seen you change their despair into hope. It's not an easy thing to go from zero to a hundred.

Whether we're talking about someone who lost their job, or looking for a new one, or simply doesn't understand the value they hold, you've shown them the way. If you can do that for someone else, then you can do anything. I know it's extremely difficult to find a way towards the light. I've been there, like most people. Luckily for me, I have you by my side at all times. For those who don't, I've always been impressed by your ability to aid them in their struggles.

I've never met anyone else who was capable of doing that. There are only two types of other individuals who could pull that off: People like Mother Theresa or Idil O. Kalif, or a person holding a law degree and were truly passionate about helping the less fortunate. Regardless of the situation, we're talking about anything ranging from simply helping someone because no one else is willing to listen to them, or individuals who might be looking for work.

Whether something ranges from small to big in terms of gravity, there's always an impact that might feel much greater than it truly is. You know that firsthand, as it's never easy for someone to believe you when you tell them they're worth just as much as anyone else. In fact, it's crazy to think that someone can see themselves as having no faith in who they are as a human being or that they possess a lower station in life than they really do. In this case, it's meant more in a proverbial manner as opposed to an actual worth of self based on where they are in life.

The lack of belief that we have in ourselves at times, is nothing more than the Shaytan telling us we can't rise above our current feeling of helplessness. When we actually believe in that, that's when we lose ourselves within a sea of despair.

For those times that you held me up and made me understand all of that, thank you. I've been able to learn a lot from you, even though you may not have realized that at the time. I know you think I don't listen to you, but it's not that I don't, it's just that I consider what you say on my own terms. It takes a while for me to ponder about what you said, as either agreeing (or disagreeing) or considering what you said, as it isn't always black and white.

Most have lost a job, a parent, a grandparent, a child and more. While others may have also lost faith in themselves, or never found their self-esteem. That being said, dealing with loss or lack of faith can feel like you're alone in the world. No one else at the time feels what you feel in the way that you feel it.

That's probably what impresses me the most about you - your ability to make sense of the situation for someone else. To be distanced enough from the situation, but close enough to understand the pain and/or frustration associated with it.

You have a natural knack for being there the way others need you to be. Sure, I've seen others do the same. The biggest difference is that you actually want to be in that position, where you're able to help them. Whereas, others are placed in that situation, feeling awkward in that moment.

All of this is what makes you more human than human. The ability to see that pain or anxiety and strive to do what you can to help them. Despite the fact that you can't be someone else and be that person, you still do what you can. The world that we live in isn't truly meant for any of us. There's always something that strives to make us miserable, which is why we have an unsatiable need to drown out that background noise.

This can range from the Qur'an to videogames, and pretty much anything. It's our way of coping with that negative chatter in the background. That in and of itself permits us to forget and ignore that there are others in this world who have nothing better to do than complain about the person we are.

In any event, we all need a ray of sunshine once in a while. Well, probably more than just once in a while. This reminds me of the term: "He/she was too beautiful for this world". To understand what that truly means is to comprehend the state of the world, and what it all encompasses. There's a lot of loss, grief, frustration, and lack of faith among a myriad of other things that depicts the nature of this world at times.

All of that leads us to understand that we don't live life, we live within it. We've all heard of the bubble boy, and that's sort of what we are. Just as much as the bubble boy can't truly live a normal life outside the bubble, that is exactly what life is for us outside the bubble. Earth itself has life on it, and we're just a grain of sand, living in this massive thing called life.

Truly, to fathom this is to understand that this life is but a mere passage for us. Whether it's fifty or a hundred years down the line, that's all it will be for us. This earth is not meant to be paradise, but it's rather meant to be the equivalent of a videogame for example. Finite. Like any videogame, it has a beginning and an end.

Hard On Yourself

The person we are hardest on is usually our own selves

With everything you've accomplished in life, as well as how you deal with people, there's certainly one thing about yourself which I wish you didn't have to go through. You are very hard on yourself, when there is no reason for you to be.

It may be true that neither of us are millionaires, nor have a successful clothing brand among a myriad of other things. However, we both have success when it comes to our talents. You definitely are too hard on yourself. I wish you weren't, as you've accomplished so much in your lifetime thus far.

We both have two degrees, which one of them is a Master's degree that you hold. That by itself is quite amazing, since most people won't obtain Master's or Doctorate degrees. As if that wasn't enough, you've improved upon your craft by being diligent. You've worked so hard to attain your goals. At any point in time, you could've easily stopped dead in your tracks, and given up or moved onto something else. But no, you opted to continue. I know I'm not the only one who's proud of you.

Both of us have more degrees than a lot of people will ever have in their lifetime. Though, degrees themselves may not directly correlate with possessing a greater level of intelligence, although it confirms so many things. From the ability to succeed in academics to the desire to help others succeed as much as you have. The fact that you paid your way [with a job] to get several degrees is a testament to your willingness to work hard.

Money is not an indicator of success per se. If anything, it's an indicator of how successful you were at convincing others that your caliber is worth more than what they pay you. That being said, you're not about that life. Instead, your worth is tied into the value you place into others, so they can succeed. For you, a mark of success is not the amount of money you make, but the success in them because of your talent to make it so.

You pride yourself in being the best person you can be, because money does not make the world go round. Rather, your ability to help others and watch out for them is your way of succeeding in this world. That mentality is admirable to say the least. To actually understand what you've understood for so long is truly a monumental achievement in and of itself.

So many people believe that success is about money, but they're completely wrong. Unless their sole job is framed within the financial world, they can't expect to make money unless they're willing to position themselves to obtain that form of success.

This is the same reason why elite athletes play for years on end. They could retire whenever they want, but they're not doing it because of the money at that point. For them, it's either about playing the game they love, or simply because they want to be as successful as they can due to their competitive nature. As for the good - yet subpar athletes that are qualified enough to play in the professional leagues - they are doing it for the money, which is why they will never be elite athletes.

I've seen you pour your heart out, so that you could make the world a better place. Even if only a fragment was affected, you still made an impact. You continue doing so, as that elusive success was never about making money, though you certainly still want it, as it helps to get ahead in other regards.

Sixth Pillar Of Islam

Strength is in the unknown

You are, not only for me but others as well, the Sixth Pillar of Islam. I wish I could show you how much of an impact you've made in my life. A lot more than you could ever imagine. I'm sorry I'm unable to show you, but hopefully this letter to you has showed you how much you mean to me, as well as to others.

I've always silently listened to you. I'm aware you think I don't listen as much as I should, but I do, I assure you. You just don't know. If anything, I've learned a lot in life because of Allah's guidance through you. I've gotten to know a lot more about myself because of your help, and that is priceless.

If not for you, I'm not sure where I'd be in life, or what I'd be doing. I've been able to accomplish two goals thus far. One being monetarily related job wise, as well as actually publishing my books through a legitimate [virtual] storefront. The fact that this is my fourth book is not something I ever envisioned before marrying you.

I might not be doing everything thus far I'd want to do, or that you might want for me, but I've still accomplished a lot with your help. I know I'm not the only one who believes the same.

Family

Strength is also in known variables

You have always said that family is important. What type of husband would I be if I didn't share their thoughts about you, with you. Know that I am not the only one who believes in you. Happy wedding anniversary!

Starting off are words from your father:

About Zeinab (#2)
All my daughters (Azizah, Zeinab, Habibah and Amirah) are a blessing! Alhamdu-lillah.

When Zeinab arrived on a cold November day in Newark NJ—a day before my own birthday. Number 1 (Azizah) was ecstatic, because she now had a baby sister. Zeinab was the second granddaughter. ... we were all happy to welcome her to the world and to our family.

Saudi Arabia:
Only a few weeks old and being not well at all, she needed surgery. At Baksh Hospital in Jeddah, Saudi Arabia, Zeinab's Palestinian surgeon's demeanor showed him to be a benevolent individual. Because it was a very complex surgery I remember him telling us in a pre-surgery conversation that he would do his best, but the outcome resided with Allah. We prayed anxiously hoping for Allah's intervention and the best outcome. Her surgeon later informed us that because the surgery was a success he shared her case with colleagues at a medical conference. In many ways Zeinab's surgery was a true test of our faith.

After the surgery Zeinab's Ethiopian maid (Hajjah Dhahabah) would carry Zeinab on her back around the house while she did some light house chores; She wrapped her in a white cotton fabric around her back, and she also spoke to Zeinab in Arabic or her native language. Zeinab didn't cry much or seemed to be lonely during the day away from her working parents. Zeinab had a happy smile when we returned home from work and she developed a healthy appetite after the surgery. It was a sign of recovery—Alhamdu-lillah!

A Curious child:

What I do remember is Zeinab's curiosity. On a summer trip to a busy shopping mall in Queens New York (where her grandparents lived) she disappeared for some time in a clothing store. It was a frightful moment for her mother and myself until we found her casually trying items in the men's section of the store—we were happy to have found her. The frightfulness now removed from our thought of losing her, also spared her from being scolded. But Zeinab's mother didn't allow that occasion and the feeling to pass so easily—she had to tell Zeinab that it was not good to walk away like that. Luckily the severity of her mother's words were tempered by her grandmother's intervention who kept things calm.

Egypt:
Zeinab attended elementary school in Cairo, Egypt. Her teachers loved her at the Cairo American School in Maa'di where she and #1 walked to school daily. I remembered that her school's baseball team never lost a game (She's a team player—always neatly dressed in her uniform and ready for action from the collective support from the sidelines). Zeinab was also a Brownie in Maa'di neighborhood where we lived. Attending Brownie meetings with her older sister Azizah, they both looked so lovely in their uniforms, although I had no idea, what they and the other girls did at the meetings, but they were both happy and never complained about anything except the annoying neighborhood stray dogs that would follow them to and from the meeting.

High School and College Years:
After returning to the USA Zeinab continued elementary school in Montclair New Jersey, by then she had a second sister Habibah (and later Amirah). Zeinab made a smooth transition to finish middle school in Princeton NJ after having lived in Cairo, Egypt and Watertown, Massachusetts. She eventually moved to Georgia. I attended Zeinab's high school graduation in Fayetteville, Georgia and later her college graduation in Atlanta, when she completed her BA degree at Georgia State University (and later her MA degree at another institution in West Georgia). Happy to see her graduate was always a thankful occasion. I believe like both of her parents (and her aunt Pat) Zeinab is driven by a personal commitment to pursue her goals and to

succeed. I believe that commitment has sustained her to be prayerful, always remembering that with Allah's intervention anything is possible.

Reflection:
On one occasion going through Heathrow airport Zeinab fell on the escalator. The blood from her cut spoiled her nice crisp outfit and she cried for a short while, but we were able to calm her down and not miss the international flight.

Zeinab was always an affable child—smiling, happy, kind, friendly loveable and caring. She retains all of these attributes as an adult—but now she has developed a natural ability and confidence to lead others and to give wise and thoughtful counsel with confidence to friends and collogues.

In many ways it's the same self-confidence she had as a curious child perhaps knowing that her parents would not abandon her and were ready to protect her. I admire her strength, and her altruism for service and her love for her faith. She is now a wife and a caring sister, daughter, and aunt with a strong protective bond toward her niece Layla and her three brothers. My lasting prayer is that Zeinab and her sisters will always be the recipient of Allah's blessing. I extend my prayers and parental love to Zeinab and her sisters.
—dad.

Now are words from a second mother to both of us:

Zeinab is an exceptional person who is very lively, sociable and very loving.

Her self confidence enables her to be forgiving and to look beyond her own personal pains. She is hard working and constantly trying to improve herself and inspire her surroundings to improve themselves as well.

I seriously have never experienced any bad feelings while dealing with her since I joined my beautiful family: The Kahera's.

I feel that God blessed Zeinab with an amazing ability through which she can encourage others and instill in them great qualities just through her actions. She does her best to make those around her happy. Such an incredible altruistic beautiful lady my Zeinab is.

As a stepmom I feel very proud to have her as a very genuine stepdaughter and a very special person for me.

I ask the Almighty Allah to bless her and grant her all that the wishes for.

Sulafa AbouSamra

I know tradition would state I continue with the oldest sister, but out of solidarity for the youngest one, please indulge yourself with words from Amirah. Power to the cadets:

First and foremost: Happy Anniversary Zeinab and Sami. May time be a space of nurturing love, bliss, and deeper connection between you two.

When Sami reached out and asked us to write, I did not know what to say. I had a number of ideas swirling on how to frame the different ways that one could ultimately say, 'I love you.'

The best way that I can think of is by reflecting on our good times. It is in the times that you would pick me up after school and we would hang out at the mall window shopping and just enjoying life. Those rides after school with the windows down, listening to music lifted my spirits after days where I felt incredibly low.

It's in those moments watching you go after your goals. We all had goals and were high achievers growing up, but you were vocal about yours particularly in your actions. From your books and vision boards to your willingness to learn from others already in your path. Whatever you went for I knew you would achieve it. (Remember that anytime you get lost or feel inadequate—you've succeeded before and you will succeed again).

It's in the times watching you navigate the world with friends of different backgrounds and identities. You appeared to see all as people first with an active role in understanding what makes each person unique and being a helper on their path to living a full life. You value friendships and showing up for them in places of joy and sorrow in their lives.

Last but not least it is in being a sister to all of us. From being the one to make us your famous omelets or buying us all matching jeans. You showed your desire to keep us together through thick and thin. If Azizah and I are the bread, then you and Beebs are the peanut butter and jelly. The internal glue of our inter generational sisterhood.

We have enjoyed watching you grow and into your state of becoming. May you be blessed in this season of becoming.

Love,
Amirah

Now are words from Habibah:

Zeinab to me is a hard working, charismatic, loving sister who wears her heart on her sleeve. She cares for people more than herself. Over the years, she has shown to all of us that she will bend over backwards for family with a sense to lift the stress and tension from their lives. She goes above and beyond to help if she can. She wants everyone to do well in life. That's the kind of sister you want. Throughout the years, it's been very challenging, but her weaknesses never stopped her from success. I pray for many blessings for the both of you. I Also pray that God will give you all the desires of your heart. Love you both.

Love, Habibah

Now are words from Azizah:

For My Sister

Happy Wedding Anniversary

What I love about Zeinab...

Is her kind spirit and her generosity. She always seeks to be her highest self and has a deep compassion for helping others reach their highest potential. She is genuine and real and has a humble nature that makes her a true believer and friend of Allah SWT. Thank you for being a great sibling and May Allah bless you to always stay curious about life and maintain your spirituality and be a good nature.

Much Love - Azizah

Now are words from my father:

Zeinab is all kinds of wonderful things: warm, caring, thoughtful, funny, joyful, independent, strong-willed, beautiful, and so on and so forth. An ace at makeup too. The first time I met her at the Dorval train station, I was very nervous. That didn't last long. After a few seconds she jumped into my arms and told me how happy she was to meet me. The most important thing to me is that she made my son Sami happy, accepting him as he is and forming a deep relationship with him. In short, Zeinab is a gentle soul.

Now are words from my mother:

You are an artistic person who inspires others, which by the same token this transfers joy to others. On top of that, it's fun to share moments with you through activities. But what I appreciate just as much if not more, is your way of obtaining useful information and listening to others. Truly, you have a big heart.

Now are words from my sister:

Z is impossible not to love.

An absolute ray of sunshine, her laugh & smile always puts you in a good mood.

From her devotion to family & loved ones, her simple honesty, her passion and wisdom, this supportive woman is a force to be reckoned with.

Her Character? Larger than life, in the best possible way.

I am so thankful to have you in my life!

Love,
Gen

P.S.: Should we even mention her fashion sense?

Now, keeping the best for last, to quote Zeinab herself, as she often tells her sister (concerning me) when I'm in the background:

Here goes the peanut gallery again!

www.ingramcontent.com/pod-product-compliance
Ingram Content Group UK Ltd.
Pitfield, Milton Keynes, MK11 3LW, UK
UKHW020416250726
13967UKWH00007B/2675

9 781777 042042